The Country of My Heart

A local guide to D. H. LAWRENCE

by

BRIDGET PUGH, M.A.

Broxtowe Borough Council
1998

Acknowledgement is made to William Heinemann Limited, Laurence Pollinger Limited and to the Estate of the late Mrs. Frieda Lawrence for permission to quote extracts from the poems and the following works of D. H. Lawrence:
The White Peacock, Sons and Lovers, The Rainbow, Women in Love, The Lost Girl, Lady Chatterley's Lover, The Virgin and the Gypsy, The Collected Short Stories, The Collier's Friday Night, The Widowing of Mrs. Holroyd, The Daughter-in-Law.

First Impression 1972

Second Impression 1974

Third Impression 1978

Second Edition 1984

Third Edition 1991

First Impression 1998

Printed for

Broxtowe Borough Council, Council Offices, Foster Avenue, Beeston, Nottingham NG9 1AB

by

Hassall & Lucking Ltd., Cross Street, Long Eaton, Nottingham

ISBN 1 873608 00 4

Foreword

This booklet is intended as a guide to the local places which D. H. Lawrence used as a background for his works.

Since the first edition of this booklet was published many new developments have taken place in Eastwood, all concerned with the increasing interest in Lawrence.

The house where Lawrence was born in 1885, 8a Victoria Street, has been restored by Browtowe Borough Council as a Museum and Information Centre and is now open to the public. 28 Garden Road has similarly been restored by the Society of Young Authors as a Museum and Study Centre and is also open on application to the Honorary Curator. See walks for details.

The D. H. Lawrence Society, locally based but with an international membership, meets regularly in Eastwood.

In the Eastwood Library there is a D. H. Lawrence Room which contains amongst other Lawrence material the unique D. H. Lawrence collection.

Professor J. T. Boulton, Head of the Department of English at the University of Birmingham, is editing Lawrence's letters for Cambridge University Press. He is anxious that the collection should be as complete as possible and would be grateful for any information about original Lawrence letters which may still be in private hands.

I should like to thank Professor David Chambers' successor, Professor A. W. Coates, for the original suggestion that I should write this booklet; the late Mr. Keith Train and Mr. Lawrence Geary for their unstinting help in its preparation; Professor James Boulton and members of the Local History Council (now Association) for reading and commenting on the manuscript; Miss Lucy Edwards for much personal help, the District Librarian of Beeston Library, and the County Librarian, and the staff of the Local Studies Section for their assistance in obtaining books and lending photographs for use in the preparation of the material; Mrs. C. Thimann for obtaining information for me, Geoffrey Phillips for his illustrations and Mrs. Brown of Moorgreen for first taking me on a Lawrence walk.

I am grateful to the Nottinghamshire Local History Association, and particularly to Lawrence Craik and John Heath for their work in the preparation of the second edition.

Photo: By courtesy of the Nottinghamshire Local Studies Library

D. H. Lawrence at Nottingham University College.

Introduction

To-day Lawrence is everywhere regarded as a bold and highly experimental writer. Perhaps the first thing one ever hears about him is something to the effect that he was the man who expounded his ideas on the nature and relationships, particularly sexual, of his characters with such frankness that *The Rainbow* was banned in 1916 on the grounds of obscenity and *Lady Chatterley's Lover,* written in 1928 was not regarded as fit for general publication until 1960, and then only after a major legal battle.

But when the society which he described and which he used as a setting for his very advanced ideas is examined it becomes apparent that it was an unusually enclosed and narrow one. His themes might range widely: by the time of his later books, he was a much-travelled man and yet the greater number of his works of fiction have an astonishingly limited background and more curiously, despite the width of his later experience, it was to this background that he returned in his last novels. So that, whatever his personal variations of mood and treatment, it seems to have been Eastwood that was the place with the most abiding influence on Lawrence's writings. As a man he might explode with peevish remarks about it. To Lawrence, the writer, it was his most important source.

In fact, one of the pleasures of Lawrence lies in the 'shock of recognition,' the sudden realization that seeing a flower, a place or an experience as he described them is more vivid than one's own vision. One has only to read his works to appreciate his skill in this form of communication. Through visiting the Lawrence countryside, one can share some part of the original experience and in so doing, appreciate afresh the artistic ability which could so directly translate images into words. There is a danger in doing this—a danger that one may seek the literal truth rather than the artistic interpretation and become involved in unproductive arguments about the accuracy of this setting or that characterization. One must remember that what one sees and talks about in the Lawrence countryside are the ingredients not the dish. And a recognition of these ingredients is only valuable in that a comparison of the originals with Lawrence's composite descriptions allows us to glimpse something of his creative powers. "Fiction is not truth certainly, but it can often approach nearer to reality than a mere recital of facts." In Lawrence's fiction we surely approach very nearly to the truth of the life of his time. Lawrence's quality as a writer lay, of course, as much in the selection as in the perception of his material. It is therefore not only in the factual truth of his descriptions, but in the discovery of the artistic purpose of his deviations from that truth that the interest of looking at D. H. Lawrence in Nottinghamshire lies.

Many of the places he wrote about have been destroyed, more are being allowed to fall into decay. There is evidence everywhere of the encroachments of the industrialization which Lawrence deplored. But there is still much left to enjoy. This booklet will have served its purpose if it enables you to find it.

Photo: By courtesy of the Nottinghamshire Local Studies Library

Brinsley Colliery, now demolished. The headstocks are to be returned to their original site at Brinsley by British Coal, Nottinghamshire County Council and Broxtowe Borough Council.

Contents

Photo: By courtesy of the Nottinghamshire Local Studies Library

Figures, reading left to right from top: Emily, George, Ernest, Ada, Mrs. Lawrence, David Herbert and Mr. Lawrence.

The Life of D. H. Lawrence

In 1875, after a relatively short acquaintance, Lydia Beardsall, a school teacher, married Arthur Lawrence, a coal miner, at St. Stephen's Church, Sneinton. Lydia Beardsall had, perhaps, not realized exactly what the life of a miner's wife would be. Her sense of shock on discovering it opened a gap between husband and wife which widened with each passing year. David Herbert Lawrence was born into their sharply divided household, in Victoria Street, Eastwood.

There were to be five children in this family. David Herbert, commonly known as Bert was the third son and fourth child. Mrs. Lawrence regarded him as sickly and doubted whether she would rear him. But despite frequent bouts of bronchitis and several dangerous illnesses he survived to become the most loved son of a mother who, disappointed in her husband, turned to her children with almost stifling intensity.

He first showed his remarkable powers by gaining one of the first county scholarships to Nottingham High School. He remained there three fairly undistinguished years, spent a few months at Haywood's Surgical Goods Factory in Castle Gate, Nottingham, as a general clerk and left this, his first employment to become a pupil teacher in Eastwood and Ilkeston. From this situation he managed by dint of scholarships and the scrimping at which he and his mother seem to have been remarkably capable, to attend a teachers' course at Nottingham University College. He qualified in 1908.

He always regarded the formal education he received as a hindrance rather than a help to his artistic development. Possibly he did at this time learn almost as much from his companions as from his teachers. His friends must have been a remarkable group in any community. They called themselves the Pagans and apart from their duties as pupil teachers and students they found time to read omnivorously; to meet regularly for discussions at the British School in Eastwood; to spend their Sunday evenings in social and political argument at the house of William Hopkin, a prominent Eastwood politician and to enjoy the stimulation of the ideas of the Rev. Robert Reid, minister of the 'Congo' (Congregational) chapel which the Lawrence family attended.

Marriage solemnized at The Parish Church in the Parish of Sneinton in the County of Nottingham

When Married	Name and Surname	Age	Condition	Rank or Profession	Residence at the time of Marriage	Father's Name and Surname	Rank or Profession of Father
Dec: 27th 1875	Arthur John Lawrence	Full	Bachelor	Mining Contractor	Brinsley	John Lawrence	Tailor
	Lydia Beardsall	Full	Spinster		John St	George Beardsall	Engineer

Married in the Parish Church according to the Rites and Ceremonies of the Established Church, after Banns by me Walter Wanstall

Arthur Lawrence
Lydia Beardsall
in the Presence of us, George Beardsall
Ellen [illegible]

Reproduced by courtesy of the Nottinghamshire Record Office

The marriage certificate of Arthur John Lawrence and Lydia Beardsall.

Photo: By courtesy of the Nottinghamshire Local Studies Library

The interior of the Congregational Chapel, Eastwood. Now demolished.

Another group which was of great significance to him at this time was the Chambers family of Haggs Farm, Greasley. Lawrence's mother and Mrs. Chambers had formed a friendship when they lived as neighbours in Eastwood. The continuance of this family friendship after the Chambers moved to their new home at Haggs meant the introduction of D. H. Lawrence to a very different kind of life. He now became familiar with the farming community that existed alongside the mining community with which, through his father, he was at least theoretically familiar. He became almost one of the Chambers family. Mr. Chambers declared "Work goes like fun when Bert's here." Mrs. Chambers reflected "I should like to be next to Bert in heaven." They were all conscious of his enormous charm and intense vitality. With the older boys Lawrence worked in the fields. He helped May, the older daughter, with her school work until, she growing beyond him, he became interested in her younger sister Jessie. Jessie was his constant companion for years and was instrumental in getting his first work published. This was a short story entitled *A Prelude* which won first prize in a Nottingham Guardian Christmas competition. The youngest son of this family was David, later better known as Professor J. D. Chambers.

It was a great break in Lawrence's life when he parted from all these friends and went as a teacher to Croydon. Helen Corke, a teacher in the district said that "He was always a foreigner after he left Eastwood." But homesick as he was, he continued writing his first novel *The*

White Peacock which he had started with the encouragement of Jessie Chambers; enjoyed the literary parties to which he was invited and embarked on his second novel *The Trespasser,* based on an experience of Helen Corke's.

In 1910 Lawrence's mother died. The following year he described as his 'sick year'. He was indeed so physically ill that he determined, on the advice of his doctor, to give up teaching. From then on he supported himself by writing. Mentally too he was overtaxed. He had suffered intensely through the months of his mother's last illness; his future was extremely uncertain; he had separated from Jessie Chambers and involved himself in an engagement with Louise Burrows, one of the Pagans. It was a difficult period.

The break from this unhappy situation came suddenly. In 1912 he eloped with Frieda Weekly, née von Richtofen, wife of a professor at University College, Nottingham and a member of a German aristocratic family. There followed a time of great literary productivity. With her he embarked, as he had for some months dreamed of doing, on two years of wandering in Europe. The expansion of his horizons was matched by the variety of the form of his work. *Sons and Lovers,* his third novel, was completed in 1912, but between then and the outbreak of war his first collection of poems *Love poems and others* was made, his first book of short stories *The Prussian Officer and other stories* was issued and his first play *The Widowing of Mrs. Holroyd* published.

Frieda and Lawrence, now married, returned to England in 1914. The war years were not happy ones for them any more than for anyone else. Lawrence half expected to be conscripted but was turned down on grounds of ill health. However, as the husband of a German woman, he was suspect and subjected to a great deal of troublesome surveillance. Worst of all, however, his novel *The Rainbow* was seized and banned on the grounds of obscenity. He continued, nonetheless with his poetry and several volumes of his verse were issued at this time.

He was disillusioned with England. The end of the war saw a new pattern emerging in his life. He had for some years wished to form a community of congenial souls in Florida. The dream faded, but the ghost of it remained with him. Somewhere in the world there must be an ideal place where he and his friends could exist in perfect amity directing their lives towards various forms of artistic activity. For the remaining ten years of his life he moved from country to country in search of such an environment. Frequently when he settled in an apparently ideal spot he wrote ecstatic letters to friends telling them to come and share his bliss. Sometimes their visits were successful, all too often they resulted in quarrels. His restlessness and intensity were difficult to live with. In an attempt to find peace he moved from Europe to Ceylon, visited Australia, almost settled in New Mexico and by 1925 was back in Europe, still wandering from country to country, but remaining chiefly in France, Germany, Italy and England. In the later years many of his moves were caused by attempts to find places which suited him from the point of view of health.

He never referred to the illness that was killing him as tuberculosis. It was always his 'bronchials'. Despite it he continued, somehow to write his poems, stories, novels, plays, critical essays and travel books. His vitality kept him alive long after his friends thought he could have lived. But on March 2nd, 1930, he died at Vence in France at the age of 44.

Town and country meet in Eastwood.

Photo: From a negative in the possession of the University of Nottingham

Eastwood

Lawrence's intensity of feeling for place is most acutely apparent in his descriptions of Eastwood and its surroundings. The nature of his feelings towards his birthplace varied with his mood and age. One can see it changing from the uncritical acceptance of childhood to the analytical rejection of early manhood and finally to the nostalgia of middle age.

Thus, when Lawrence first left Eastwood for Croydon as a young man he was appalled at his own homesickness. He had not realized how deeply he was attached to his home. Later, shortly after his mother's death, when he was at odds with all the world, he exclaimed that he had always disliked the place. Yet in 1918, he wrote to an artist friend, Max Gertler, "We are spending a day in the place where I was born—Eastwood. For the first time in my life I feel quite amiably towards it. I have always hated it. Now I don't". Later still in his essay *Nottingham and the Mining Country* he fulminated against Eastwood's "ugliness, ugliness, ugliness," pointing out how such surroundings stunted the souls of those who lived there and asking why "those sordid and hideous Squares" built by the mine-owners for their workers on Victoria Street and Albert Street could not have been modelled on an Italian village with a piazza to instil some focus of community.

Yet this criticism of Eastwood, born of his experiences of other towns throughout the world was accompanied by a romanticization of the area. Eastwood and its wider neighbourhood were, he declared "the real England—the hard pith of England". "For me, as a young boy," he wrote, "it was still the old England of the forest and the agricultural past; there were no motor cars, the mines were, in a sense, an accident in the landscape and Robin Hood and his merry men were not far away." "The mill only ceased grinding the local corn when I was a child. And my father, who always worked in Brinsley pit and who always got up at 5 o'clock, if not at four, would set off in the dawn across the fields at Coney Grey and hunt for mushrooms in the long grass or perhaps pick up a skulking rabbit which he would bring home at evening inside the lining of his pit coat."

These remarks show the changing attitudes of the man. The attitude of the writer is rather different, for a writer has to use his material for the purpose of his art rather than merely to convey personal feelings. In Eastwood, Lawrence had a ready-made background for his work. What he thought about Eastwood was not nearly as important as what he knew about it. From this knowledge he could recreate a community in his books, Eastwood for Lawrence, the writer, was matter for description, rather than direct social criticism.

The beginning of *The Lost Girl* illustrates this. Lawrence was personally deeply moved by social inequalities, but in this passage he notes them quite impersonally. "Here we are then; a vast substratum of colliers; a thick sprinkling of tradespeople intermingled with small employers of labour and diversified by elementary school teachers and non-conformist clergy; a higher layer of bank managers, rich millers and well-to-do ironmasters, episcopal clergy and the managers of collieries; then the rich and sticky cherry of the local coal owner glistening over all.

Such is the complicated social system of a small industrial town in the Midlands of England."

In his novels, Lawrence was concerned with depicting, not analysing, the life of Eastwood and the gay panorama of the weekly market and the twice-yearly fairs mingle with daily routine to make the community spring again to life as it existed at the turn of the century.

The market was a great event. We learn in the partly autobiographical novel *Sons and Lovers* how "Mrs. Morel loved her marketing. In the tiny market place on the top of the hill, where four roads from Nottingham and Derby, Ilkeston and Mansfield, meet, many stalls were erected. Brakes ran in from surrounding villages. The market place was full of women, the streets packed with men. It was amazing to see so many men everywhere in the streets. Mrs. Morel usually quarrelled with her lace woman, sympathized with her fruit man—who was a gaby, but his wife was a bad un—laughed with the fish-man—who was a scamp, but so droll—put the linoleum man in his place, was cold with the odd-wares man, and only went to the crockery man when she was driven—or drawn by the cornflowers on a little dish." The passage continues with an account of her bargaining for this dish for which she paid fivepence and returning home to explain "I'm a wicked, extravagant woman. I know I s'll come to want."

With similar vividness Lawrence described his father making fuses for use in the mine. "Morel fetched a sheaf of long sound wheatstraws from the attic. These he cleaned with his hand, till each one gleamed like a stalk of gold, after which he cut the straws into lengths of about six inches, leaving, if he could, a notch at the bottom of each piece. He always had a beautifully sharp knife that could cut a straw clean without hurting it. Then he set in the middle of the table a heap of gunpowder, a little pile of black grains upon the white-scrubbed board. He made and trimmed the straws while Paul and Annie filled and plugged them. Paul loved to see the black grains trickle down a crack in his palm into the mouth of the straw, peppering jollily downwards till the straw was full. Then he bunged up the mouth with a bit of soap, which he got in his thumb-nail from a pat in the saucer—and the straw was finished."

These direct descriptions make the reader share the life of Lawrence's characters. He uses the same direct technique in his impersonal account of the Squares in *Sons and Lovers*—"To accommodate the regiments of miners, Carson, Waite and Co. built the Squares, great quadrangles of dwellings on the hillside." Lawrence was born at 8a Victoria Street, in this area. A plaque over the door marks the house which is now a museum. His mother disliked the place and Lawrence's remarks on its ugliness which were quoted earlier shows what he thought of it. But as a writer it was not appropriate

Drawn by Geoffrey Phillips

Lawrence's birthplace and museum, 8a Victoria Street, Eastwood.

Photo: *By courtesy of the Nottinghamshire Local Studies Library*

The house in the Breach.

to his art to make explicit any criticism of the area which was a home to his characters.

The same relatively neutral form of description is to be found in his account of the second Lawrence home which also occurs in *'Sons and Lovers'.* This is the house in the Breach, now number 28 Garden Road. Lawrence wrote "The houses themselves were substantial and very decent. One could walk all around seeing little front gardens with auriculas and saxifrage in the shadow of the bottom block, sweet williams and pinks in the sunny top block; seeing neat front windows, little porches. But that was outside; that was the view on to the uninhabited parlours of all the colliers' wives. The dwelling room, the kitchen was at the back of the house, facing inward between the blocks looking at a scrubby back garden and then at the ash pits. And between the rows, between the long lines of ash pits, went the alley, where the children played and the women gossiped and the men smoked. So the actual conditions of living in the Bottoms, that was so well built and looked so nice were quite unsavoury because people must live in the kitchen and the kitchen opened on to that nasty alley of ash pits."

Drawn by Geoffrey Phillips

The Walker Street house.

These are the remarks of one who has lived in a house and experienced its drawbacks. They illustrate Lawrence's quality of taking his reader straight into an experience of life instead of leaving him as an observer. Most important, in their omission of any overt reference to the lack of understanding which allowed these homes to be built in this way, they illustrate Lawrence's power of selection, his writer's detachment which allows him to use for his work only what is necessary to his purpose. We know he felt strongly about the divisions between rich and poor. Here his feelings were not relevant.

After living in the Breach, the Lawrences moved to the third house in Walker Street. Jessie Chambers recalled that Lawrence nick-named it 'Bleak House', because it stood open to the winds. She added "They had a wide view over the houses in the valley to the meadows beyond, and to where High Park wood began. Lawrence has told me how he used to watch the cloud shadows stalking across the fields."

In 1902 the Lawrences moved again to a house in Lynn Croft Road, now number 97. It was yet another move upward socially for they passed from a terraced house to a semi-detached one. Jessie Chambers remarked that Lawrence was proud of his new home which "had a little entrance hall, with the stairs and the doors to the other rooms going out from it. There was a cooking range in the scullery as well as in the living-room, a china closet in addition to the pantry, a cupboard under the side windows where the school books were kept, and from the big window of the living room was the view over the roofs of Eastwood to the square church tower standing high above."

In considering the four Lawrence homes we see the real roots of the writer's connection with Eastwood. These houses were a part of Lawrence's life and he used them also in his writings. Lawrence, more than many writers, was involved in and evolved from his childhood locality. It was the fabric of his early life and the abiding quality of his books comes largely from the directness of his description of the place. He felt it of himself and wrote of it as such.

It was a pity that he wrote in such a manner as to make himself personally unpopular there. For, of course, he wrote not only about Eastwood as a place, but about Eastwood as a community of people. And just as people recognised the places he wrote about so too they recognized themselves and others in his characters. But the same thing holds true for his descriptions of people as it does for his account of places. They are a starting ground. Within the background of Eastwood a story evolves: within the physical description of one person a quite different character is developed. And if the true and fictitious characters even experience the same events their reactions are different enough to show how the part they play if not the appearance they present in Lawrence's works is chiefly his invention.

We cannot leave Eastwood without saying something about the surrounding countryside which was quite as important to Lawrence as the town itself.

It was in 1926 that he wrote about it in an oft-quoted letter to Rolf Gardiner where he exclaimed: "How well I can see Hucknall Torkard and the miners! Didn't you go into the church to see the tablet, where Byron's heart is buried? My father used to sing in the Newstead Abbey choir, as a boy. But I've gone many times down Hucknall Long Lane to Watnall—and I like Watnall Park—it's a great Sunday morning walk. Some of my happiest days I've spent haymaking in the fields just opposite the south side of Greasley church—bottom of Watnall Hill—adjoining the vicarage: Miriam's father hired those fields. If you're in those parts again, go to Eastwood, where I was born and lived for my first 21 years. Go to Walker Street and stand in front of the third house—and look across at Crich on the left, Underwood in front—High Park woods and Annesley on the right: I lived in that house from the age of 6 to 18, and I know that view better than any in the world. Then walk down the fields to the Breach, and in the corner house facing the stile I lived from 1 to 6. And walk up Engine Lane, over the level crossing at Moorgreen pit, along till you come to the highway (the Alfreton Road)—turn to the left, towards Underwood, and go till you come to the lodge gate by the reservoir—go through the gate and up the drive to the next gate, and continue on the footpath just below the drive on the left—on through the wood to Felley Mill (the White Peacock farm). When you've crossed the brook, turn to the right through Felley Mill gate, and go up the footpath to Annesley. Or better still, turn to the right uphill, before you descend to the brook, and go on uphill, up the rough deserted pasture—on past Annesley Kennels—long empty—on to Annesley again. That's the country of my heart. From the hills, if you look across at Underwood wood, you'll see a tiny red farm on the edge of the wood. That was Miriam's farm—where I got my first incentive to write." The Miriam of whom he spoke was the fictionalized representation of Jessie Chambers in *Sons and Lovers;* the farm, The Haggs.

It is not difficult to imagine the sense of joy and liberation the boy from Eastwood must have felt in exploring this countryside. We shall look elsewhere and in detail at the use Lawrence made of it in his novels. Broadly speaking, it combines a quite extraordinary sensitivity of observation with such familiar knowledge that his accounts of the places he knew enable the reader to feel that he is almost a participant in any scene rather than a mere observer. At the same time the Eastwood country that Lawrence describes is often subtly altered from the literal truth. Distances extend and diminish, houses do the same. The Lawrence country of fact is unexpectedly beautiful as you will find if you go there. The Lawrence country of fiction is beautifully presented. There is a difference.

Felley Mill Farm

Photo: By courtesy of the Nottinghamshire Local Studies Library

Nottingham

Today Eastwood seems almost a suburb of Nottingham, at least to a stranger driving from one to the other. It was very different in Lawrence's time. Then the city and the town had quite separate identities and the nine miles between the two kept them apart. Men, like the miners in *Strike Pay,* might make an excursion to a football match, but the women and children of Eastwood tended to stay at home unless involved in a major shopping expedition for furniture or trousseaux.

Lawrence's works emphasise this division. This may have been because his own knowledge of Nottingham was confined to the districts in which he studied and worked, the areas around the High School, the old University College, now part of the Trent Polytechnic in Shakespeare Street and the streets around the Castle. Certainly the fact that he had to send Jessie Chambers to Basford Registry Office to see what it looked like before describing it in *The White Peacock* suggested no very wide knowledge of the town. But more probably, at least in his early works there was a clear artistic purpose in separating Nottingham from Eastwood.

If one reads about George Saxton's journey into Nottingham with his bride-to-be, Meg, this purpose becomes clear. The whole account is studded with references to buildings of local note: "The square tower of my old school (the High School) and the sharp proud spire of St. Andrews"; "Basford, where the swollen gasometers stood like toadstools; the Castle with below it 'the sun sloping over the great river flats'; Colwick Park, the Trent Bridges; the Theatre Royal and the Victoria Hotel." The effect of this commentary on these, to them unfamiliar, buildings is to turn the outing into a spree. The travellers are visiting new country and are exhilarated by it.

The same impression of strangeness appears when Paul Morel in *Sons and Lovers* feels that looking for the firm for which he was going to work was "like hunting in some wild place." Here the boy's natural tension is emphasized by the unfamiliarity of the setting.

In his later works, however, where his characters were assured enough to move easily in a more sophisticated atmosphere than Eastwood, Lawrence shows that he is as skilful in describing places in Nottingham as in Eastwood. Thus in *The Rainbow* we read of the old University College in the words "She liked the hall with its big stone chimney piece and its Gothic arches supporting the balcony above. To be sure the arches were ugly, the chimney-piece of cardboard-like carved stone with its armorial decoration looked silly just opposite the bicycle stand and the radiator, whilst the great notice board with the fluttering papers seemed to slam away all sense of retreat and mystery from the far wall. Nevertheless, amorphous as it might be, there was in it a reminiscence of the wondrous, cloistral origin of education."

Lawrence's descriptions of Nottingham thus show an interesting opening-out which might indeed suggest a parallel development in Lawrence himself.

The Novels

There are eight novels which, by virtue of their setting, come within the scope of a booklet about Lawrence and Nottinghamshire: *The White Peacock* published in 1911; *Sons and Lovers,* 1913; *The Rainbow,* 1915; *Women in Love,* 1920; *The Lost Girl,* 1920; *Aaron's Rod,* 1922; *Lady Chatterley's Lover,* 1928; and *The Virgin and the Gypsy,* 1930.

The novel as an art form is always concerned with personality and most frequently with personality as revealed through social relationships. Lawrence looked deeper, he was concerned with the basis of personality; the hidden springs of the subconscious, the intangible links between one human being and another. The search for what fulfils or destroys character at its very deepest level is the common theme of these novels we are looking at.

Lawrence links this theme with the changing nature of the Midland countryside in the first quarter of the century. He saw the invasion of the landscape by the ugliness of industrialism, as a reflection of the destruction of natural man removed from his instinctive communion with the rest of the universe by the banalities of Board School eductation, the social ambitions of his women-folk and mechanization.

One of the symbols he uses for this is the mine—the form of industrialism with which he, in Eastwood, would have been most familiar. He saw the mine, where men had formerly worked in a community, become a formidable soul-destroying machine.

He came to the conclusion eventually that the only hope for mankind lay in the escape from the materialism and acquisitiveness of an industrial society to the freer life of an earlier time. It was perhaps this conclusion which led him to return to a visionary Midland setting for his later unfinished dream fictions—to Lathkill Dale in *The Flying Fish* and Eastwood in *A Dream of Life.*

The White Peacock

At the beginning of this book, Lettie, a young, capricious middle class girl amuses herself by rousing George, a farmer's son from his complacent ignorance of a world wider than his experience although she intends to marry Lesley Tempest, a mine-owner's son. There is a moment of balance early in the novel where it almost seems that she might marry George. But she feels him beneath her, marries Lesley and leaves George to marry Meg, the barmaid. The book ends with the dissolution of George. He is ostensibly destroyed by the demon drink, but the roots of his destruction lie in his separation from the old life of the land and Lettie's denial of their affinity. Lettie's life is sterile because of this same denial.

It is interesting that Professor Chambers in discussing the book immediately recognised Lettie as Ada Lawrence, later Clarke, and George as his brother Alan. One can mention a few other such connections. Lesley Tempest is the first of the long series of mine-owner's sons whom Lawrence is said to have based on members of the

---

Photo: By courtesy of London Screen Distributors

Left. Joanna Shimkus and Franco Nero in a scene from D. H. Lawrence's 'The Virgin and The Gypsy'.

Barber family without any personal knowledge of the family to guide him. The group of young people represent members of the Pagans. The gamekeeper Annable had his origin in another gamekeeper Naylor, also known to Professor Chambers, though there is no suggestion that they were alike in character.

Plot and characterization are not, however, the most significant aspects of the book. The outstanding feature of this first novel is the evocation of the countryside around Eastwood. One has only to read the description of flowers in a wet May to appreciate the freshness of its natural detail "the light of the dandelions was quite extinguished, and it seemed that only a long time back had we made merry before the broad glare of these flowers. The bluebells lingered and lingered; they fringed the fields for weeks like purple fringe of morning. The pink campions came out only to hang heavy with rain; hawthorn buds remained tight and hard as pearls."

Photo: Lawrence Geary

The Haggs.

The centre of the countryside was, of course, The Haggs. Professor J. D. Chambers in his *Memoir of D. H. Lawrence,* published in *Renaissance and Modern Studies, Oct.* 72, described Lawrence as having a love affair "with the little farm house clothed in Virginia creeper and honeysuckle, with the old mare, Flower, who leaned over the garden fence and nibbled the roses, the good-natured bull terrier Trip who lay across the hearth in front of the fire; and there were two massive old sows to whom he gave classical names: one a cheerful chubby creature with twinkling blue eyes always ready to hold up her snout for an apple he called Dido; the other, a long lean lugubrious creature, always complaining and never satisfied he called Circe." Here one glimpses some of the source material of *The White Peacock* where Trip appears under his own name and even the sows have their part.

Elsewhere Professor Chambers recalled some of the activities of the young people who met at The Haggs, "all the usual party games, but above all we played charades . . . Lawrence, of course, was the moving spirit. I remember he was especially fond of dressing up my brother Alan in some oriental costume . . . and I can see him standing back and admiring my brother's display of tanned neck and arms". Readers of *The White Peacock* can immediately see the connection between the scenes of Professor Chamber's reminiscences and scenes in the book. Lawrence was writing directly from experience.

Even the topography of the novel is easy to identify if one looks at a map of Eastwood. 'The Ram Inn' is still to be seen on the Moorgreen Road, although the inn Lawrence must have known was situated where there is now a private dwelling opposite a palatial new Ram Inn. Lambclose House probably suggested Highclose in *The White Peacock.* Woodside, Professor Chambers thought, was 'the Keeper's Lodge on the wood leading alongside Nethermere (Moorgreen Reservoir) to Strelley but it may have been the shooting lodge Beauvale House'. The quarry where Annable died is thought to have been at Willeywood Farm and the church where the white peacock appeared was the old church in Annesley Park.

The church is still standing—a ruin as it was in Lawrence's day and too dangerous to visit. But alongside it the road is recognisable as the one Lawrence knew when he wrote "So I left the wild lands, and went along by the old red wall of the kitchen garden, along the main road as far as the mouldering church which stands high on a bank by the roadside just where the trees tunnel the darkness and the gloom of the highway startles the traveller at noon. Great trees growing on the banks suddenly fold over everything at this point in the swinging road, and in the obscurity rots the Hall church, black and melancholy above the shrinking head of the traveller."

This has changed little. But it is sad to visit Felley Mill—the Strelley Mill of *The White Peacock*—and to see it has been demolished. Above it, however, one can see the mill pond of which Lawrence writes and the place where the 'thin stream' used to fall through the millrace. This, at least, cannot be spoiled.

Cossethay in this book has almshouses similar to those in Cossall.

Sons and Lovers

The same use of actual places as the setting for the story is to be found in *Sons and Lovers.* As we have seen Eastwood is important at the beginning of the book. The houses of Lawrence's childhood all appear, the places where he played, The Sun Inn and The Three Tuns where his father drank. It was a slightly different landscape from the one one might see now. Beauvale Brook still ran clear through the country below the Breach. There were open fields where the children could play, wide expanses of country in which to go blackberrying. But it is still recognisable.

The area around The Haggs reappears as Willey Farm. Lawrence's intimate knowledge of the house, the garden and the fields is once more apparent here. Nethermere on "a glistening, white-and-blue day", Strelley Mill Farm and Willey Water, the mill pond, form a background to and are part of the life of the characters.

Beyond all this lies the life of the mine—the life his father knew well and which he uses as his material in both his plays and short stories. It appears as a life entirely masculine, with its own taboos, its own communal spirit. It is described with such accuracy that the actual mines around Eastwood are each differentiated "Spinney Park is High Park; Minton is Moorgreen; Beggarlee is Brinsley; Selby is Selston; Watnall is Nuttall and Bunker's Hill is Butler's Hill".

A striking thing which emerges from the book is Lawrence's appreciation of the beauty of the pits. Clara Dawes comments "What a pity there is a coal pit here, where it is so pretty!" Paul Morel (Lawrence) replied "Do you think so? You see I am so used to it I should miss it. No; and I like the pits here and there. I like the rows of trucks, and the headstocks, and the stream in the daytime, and the lights at night. When I was a boy, I always thought a pillar of cloud by day and a pillar of fire by night was a pit, with its steam, and its lights, and the burning bank and I thought the Lord was always at the pit-top." At this time, of course, we must remember that the countryside was not as disfigured with slag heaps as it is now. In fact, Brinsley pit did not have one at all.

Lawrence showed a similar appreciation of the dramatic effect of the little railways winding from Nottingham and of the main line with its trains rushing between such far off places as London and Scotland.

His seeing eye extends to the warehouse in Nottingham where he was first employed. Jordan's as it is called in *Sons and Lovers* was "a big warehouse, with creamy paper parcels everywhere, and clerks, with their shirt sleeves rolled back—going about in an at-home sort of way. The light was subdued, the glossy cream parcels seemed luminous, the counters were of dark brown wood."

Photo: By courtesy of the Nottinghamshire Local Studies Library

Jessie Chambers upon whom Miriam in 'Sons and Lovers' was based. Compare a contemporary photograph of Lawrence on page 4 with this and the glamorised film version opposite.

The descriptions of working conditions here bring one to a sharp realization of how much working conditions have altered in the last seventy years. Paul Morel worked a twelve hour day and at the end of it faced a seven-mile train journey and a two mile walk home. For this he earned eight shillings a week. And his situation was better than that of Clara Dawes, trimming and carding lace in a 'mean little street' near Bluebell Hill or that of his mother's neighbours sewing up twenty-four undyed stockings for 'two-pence ha'penny'.

At least in *Sons and Lovers* social injustice does not appear to affect him. Social commentary, in fact, only appears as a vehicle for revelation of character. Indeed the book is full of cheerfulness and gaiety, of holiday expeditions which must have been singularly memorable in a life of such drudgery.

The longest journeys took Paul Morel to the Isle of Wight, to Skegness and the seaside at Mablethorpe in Lincolnshire. Shorter ones included the excursion to Wingfield Manor. This involved a train journey from Langley Mill to Alfreton, a visit to the church there, an exploration of the manor with its 'winding staircase', 'high tower' and crypt 'in perfect preservation' and a long walk through Crich and Whatstandwell to Ambergate where another train took them home. Another expedition took him and his friends to the Hemlock Stone, through Ilkeston, Stanton Gate and Trowell. "They had expected a

Photo: Reproduction by courtesy of Twentieth Century Fox Film Company Limited

Paul and Miriam as portrayed by Dean Stockwell and Heather Sears in the film of 'Sons and Lovers'.

venerable and dignified monument. They found a little, gnarled, twisted stump of rock, something like a decayed mushroom, standing out pathetically on the side of a field." Both these trips occurred in fact according to Ada Clarke.

Another one which might or might not have been fictitious was the walk taken by Paul Morel and Clara Dawes from the Trent past Wilford churchyard and Clifton Grove to Clifton village.

Even the story of the novel is a version of Lawrence's own life. He wrote "It follows this idea: a woman of character and refinement goes into the lower class, and has no satisfaction in her own life. She has had a passion for her husband, so the children are born of passion and have heaps of vitality. But as her sons grow up she selects them as lovers—first the eldest, then the second. These sons are urged into life by their reciprocal love of their mother—urged on and on. But when they come to manhood, they can't love, because their mother is the strongest power in their lives, and holds them. . . . As soon as the young men come into contact with women, there's a split. William gives his sex to a fribble, and his mother holds his soul. But the split kills him because he doesn't know where he is. The next son gets a woman who fights for his soul—fights his mother. The son loves the mother—all the sons hate and are jealous of the father. The battle goes on between the mother and girl with the son as object. The mother gradually proves stronger because of the tie of blood. The son decides to leave his soul in his mother's hands, and, like his elder brother, go for passion. He gets passion. Then the split begins to tell again. But, almost unconsciously, the mother realizes what is the matter, and begins to die. The son casts off his mistress, attends to his mother dying. He is left in the end naked of everything, with the drift towards death."

The raw materials of this book were taken from real life and were recognisable as such. The Lawrences suggested the Morels; the Chambers, the Leivers; the Pagans, the crowd of young people connected with the two families; the Barbers the mine-owners, and several women of his acquaintance, the many-sided Clara Dawes.

But it is quite as interesting to look at the places where the book departs from factual truth as to trace where it recounts it, because most people, when they read *Sons and Lovers* regard it purely as an autobiography and this it is not. It is an autobiographical novel with a theme and development of pattern quite foreign to the formlessness of life. Let us look at some of the more obvious divergences between fact and fiction in the novel.

The most obvious difference lies in making Paul Morel an artist instead of a writer, thus taking up Lawrence's other talent for painting instead of his main one of writing.

There must have been some truth in Lawrence's account of the strained relationship between his father and mother. But he certainly heightened it in order to achieve his desired artistic effect. He heightened it first by exaggerating the social difference in his parents' origins—they were connected by marriage and the father did not come from a background materially much inferior to that of his wife. In addition to this Lawrence diminished his father in the book by only allowing rare glimpses of the vitality and gaiety for which he was well-known locally to appear. It was essential in the book that the father should be a morose drunkard, a 'poor provider' in order to throw the mother's heroism into relief and to make her more dependent on and therefore, more possessive of her boys.

In the same way Lawrence re-arranged his family and that of the Chambers to make the scope of his book more manageable. In his poem *Monologue of a Mother* he describes his mother as losing three sons to the world outside. In *Sons and Lovers* only two are significant, though the story follows truth closely in recounting the death of the older boy and the serious illness of Lawrence himself. There is only one daughter, Annie. Similarly he describes the Leivers family as smaller than the Chambers one was. There were seven children in the Chambers family. In *Sons and Lovers* only five appear.

Moreover, he arranges the events of his own life to make them more acceptable artistically. The book gives the impression that he was largely self-educated and that his life followed the normal pattern of a working class boy of his time in passing straight from Board School to employment, in his case as a clerk in a Surgical Goods Factory in Nottingham. It also suggests that he remained employed in this way. In actual fact he only remained as a clerk for three months and then resumed his education. He also gave the impression in the book that the girls at the factory were pleasant and amiably disposed towards him. But William Hopkin recalled that in reality they were a coarse and unpleasant group. Both these alterations have a significant effect—the first because Paul Morel's lack of education and consequently narrower horizons made his susceptibility to the domination of his womenfolk more comprehensible. The second because it suggests a greater innocence on Paul's part—an innocence which would have the same effect as his narrowness of education.

These alterations hurt no one, for his father, to whom Lawrence later admitted he had been unjust, could not read what his son had said about him. His account of the story of his relationship with the Chambers family, was a different matter however.

His detailed description of the intimacies of their family life, the burned potatoes, the wrangling amongst the children, the dirty aprons and the broken shoes were, in a sense, a betrayal of their friendship. And one can understand the hurt which Jessie Chambers must have felt in seeing her cherished friendship used as material for a book in a way which seemed to her a travesty of the truth even though she herself had suggested that Lawrence's original version should be re-cast 'closer to life.'

But these are moral judgments and although it is tempting to make them (as Jessie found in her *Personal Record* of Lawrence) what is important in a consideration of the book is whether his use of his material was effective. And one must admit that his writings gain immeasurably from the portraits based on the people he knew and the descriptions of familiar places.

The Rainbow and *Women in Love*

The Rainbow and *Women in Love* continue this use of real people and real places although, at least in the first book, the main protagonists come from a different family and their setting is a new one.

The structure of the two books may summed up as being a survey, particularly in their marriage relationships, of several generations of one

family which narrows itself to concentrate on the coming to personal maturity of two of the daughters of the generation contemporary with Lawrence.

The part of the family—the Brangwen family—with which Lawrence was most closely concerned—was, as Professor Boulton has pointed out in *Lawrence in Love,* suggested by the Burrows family. Lawrence was engaged to Louise Burrows at the time of his mother's death and came to know her parents well. Like so many of Lawrence's friends they served as models for his current book.

Alfred Burrows (Louise's father) and William Brangwen are remarkably similar. Alfred Burrows was passionately interested in his local church at Cossall where he was choirmaster and looked after the fabric and furnishings. William Brangwen "worked for many years at Cossethay, building the organ for the church, restoring the woodwork." Alfred Burrows had a twice-weekly evening class in the village school and taught handicrafts. Eventually he gave up his job as a lace designer to become peripatetic teacher of handicrafts in Leicestershire. William Brangwen made a similar move.

Lawrence even showed Brangwen as living in Church Cottage, Cossall, the very house in which Burrows brought up his family. "It was the cottage next the church, with dark yew trees, very black old trees, along the side of the house and grassy front garden; a red squarish cottage with a low slate roof, and low windows. It had a long dairy scullery, a big flagged kitchen and a low parlour that went up one step from the kitchen. There were white-washed beams across the ceilings, and odd corners with cupboards. Looking out through the windows there was the grassy garden, the procession of black yew trees down one side and along the other sides, a red wall with ivy separating the place from the high road and the church yard. The little, old church with its small spire on a square tower seemed to be looking back at the cottage windows," The cottage is called Yew Tree Cottage in the book.

Drawn by Geoffrey Phillips

Church Cottage, Cossall.

Lawrence used another house in Cossall as the home of previous generations of Brangwens. This was Marsh Farm. It is now completely demolished, but one can see the site under the new bungalow, Pipswood, just under the railway line, on one's right as one turns from Cossall to Ilkeston. Here one can still imagine the place as Lawrence described it, cut off from the industrial world but reminded of it by sounds from over the hill. In his day it was the 'clink, clink, clink' of the now disused colliery. Today the traffic on the road below provides a similar disturbance. Yet if one explores the footpaths in the Cossall

---

Left. Louise Burrows.

Photo: By courtesy of Professor J. T. Boulton

Photo: By courtesy of the Nottinghamshire Local Studies Library

Lambclose House. The home of the Barber Family.

Kimberley, Strelley area one finds a quiet landscape that must have changed little in a century.

In *Women in Love,* however, one leaves this countryside for the already familiar setting of the woods and fields around Eastwood. The Haggs is no longer the centre—its place is taken by Shortlands "a long, low, old house, a sort of manor farm that spread along the top of a slope just beyond the narrow little lake of Willey Water". We return again, in fact, to Lambclose house and Moorgreen Reservoir.

The social milieu of the book has also changed. Louise Burrows, 'churchy' and passionate may have served as a model for Ursula Brangwen, the elder of the two sisters on whom *Women in Love* concentrates. Here she is endowed with an artistic gift which gives her, as it gave Lawrence himself, an entree into wealthy families whom she might not otherwise have known.

So we return to the mine-owning family with which Lawrence appears to have been infatuated—the Barbers—in the book called Crich. Lawrence even went so far as to include in his book two Barber family tragedies—the accidental shooting of one of the sons by another and the drowning of one of the daughters and her would-be rescuer in Moorgreen Reservoir.

Such are the local connections in the two books, connections which provide a vehicle for an enormously complicated survey of Midland society at the beginning of this century.

The Lost Girl

The Lost Girl starts in urban Eastwood and Langley Mill and ends in the mountains of Italy. In one sense it traces Lawrence's own progress. But at least at the beginning, it reflects also the history of a 'well-respected' family in Eastwood though it soon departs from any real connection with them as far as character goes.

The setting of the story was London House, a draper's shop in Eastwood's main street, now a modern building 50m on from Victoria Street. This Lawrence called Manchester House. The Cambridge edition of *The Lost Girl* notes, as described in the book, that there is a side entrance to the shop in Albert Street. It identifies Parker's Picture Palace (Wright's Cinematograph and Variety Theatre) as lying just below the Sun Inn on the Langley Mill road and places the Empire Theatre at the junction of Wellington Road and the High Road. It also suggests that Alvina's walk from the Congregational Chapel went through the allotments above the Breach, along the mineral railway and up the Mansfield Road. (See the map for Walk 1).

The owner of the shop had a career which had something in common with that of the James Houghton of the novel. Both of them at one time owned a small coal mine "Throttle Ha'penny" in Eastwood on Connection Meadow behind the Methodist New Connection Chapel. Lawrence had, apparently, always been welcome in the household. He knew it well and described it accurately. Of course his account is not exact. There is only one daughter in his book although there were were, in fact, two. They were taught by a private governess Miss Wright, according to Ada Clarke "a splendid woman who stayed with the family until she died. She made a comfortable living teaching music." Mrs. Clarke also added that "she spared no pains in helping Bert in his education." Miss Wright became the Miss Frost of the book.

Eastwood is called Woodhouse in *The Lost Girl.* Langley Mill also appears under the name of Lumley. The description is not flattering. "It has a long straggle of a dusty road down in the valley, with a pale grey dust and spatter from the pottery, and big chimneys bellying forth black smoke right by the road. Then there was a short cross-way, up which one saw the iron foundry, a black and rusty place. A little further on was the railway junction and beyond that more houses stretching to Hathersedge, where the stocking factories were busy. Compared with Lumley, Woodhouse, whose church could be seen sticking up proudly and vulgarly as an eminence, above trees and meadow-slopes, was an idyllic heaven."

Aaron's Rod

Aaron's Rod like *The Lost Girl* starts in Eastwood but very quickly moves away. The Eastwood Lawrence describes here is Eastwood 'after the war' and is characterized by a greedy pre-Christmas rush which he disliked. The little market at the top of the town appears to have gone. Goods are in short supply. It is very different from Mrs. Morel's Eastwood.

Aaron Sisson, the hero of the book, bears a marked resemblance to descriptions of the Lawrence's next door neighbour in Lynn Croft Road, a checkweighman, interested in music and physically fair and robust. Certainly the house described at the beginning of the book resembles the Lynn Croft house.

Aaron is accurately described as returning from work to it from the little black railway line, over a stile, a field and another stile to the long road of colliers' dwellings.

The house that was the model for Shottle House is now demolished. It lay on the left of the Mansfield Road and along Cockerhouse Road, or as Lawrence called it Shottle House Road. The now disused Plumptre Colliery alongside this road Lawrence renamed New Brunswick Colliery. Further down the Mansfield Road, on the right was The Royal Oak, an inn Lawrence described as The Thorn Tree.

Lady Chatterley's Lover

It is fairly widely accepted locally that Lady Chatterley's Lover is set in Eastwood with the familiar Lambclose House, now re-named Wragby Hall. Eastwood people refer to the game-keeper's cottage as one of the huts now used by woodsmen on the estate.

Certainly in his second version of the book Lawrence referred to the Eastwood country. Mark Schorer wrote "There, late in the novel, Lawrence has his lovers go to the Eastwood country; they meet in the church at Hucknall where 'the pinch of dust that was Byron's heart (Byron, that fat lad!)' is enshrined, and they survey the old Lawrence landscape—Haggs Farm now deserted. Felley Mill still and abandoned, everything 'dead as Nineveh', all life sacrificed to 'coal and iron'."

Yet it is also clear that this book sprang from his return to the Midlands in 1925 and particularly 1926 and that it was touched off partly by his hatred of the damage that he saw industrialism doing there.

All his descriptions of places in *Lady Chatterley's Lover* are jaundiced. As far as the identification of localities is concerned Wragby appears very like Renishaw the Sitwell home near Sheffield. Both the description of the house: "a long low old house in brown stone, begun about the middle of the eighteenth century, and added on to, till it was a warren of a place without much distinction", and its setting: "It stood on an eminence in a rather fine old path of oak trees, but alas, one could see in the near distance the chimney of Tevershall pit, with its clouds of steam and smoke", suggests that Lawrence had Renishaw in mind here. So too does the situation of the church which in the book and in fact stands opposite the house.

The journey which Constance Chatterley took "travelling south" past Bolsover Castle (Warsop in the book), Staveley (Stack Gates), Hardwick (Chadwick Hall) to Chesterfield (Uthwaite) and back through the Dukeries where Fritchley is probably Sutton Scarsdale Hall and Shipley is not unlike Barlborough, suggests that Lawrence envisages the house in the same geographical position as Renishaw. So too does the description of Connie seeing steel workers from Sheffield . . . off for an excursion to Matlock.

But it is difficult to decide whether, in thinking of the village Tevershall, Lawrence was recreating Eckington or Eastwood. "The car ploughed uphill through the long squalid straggle of Tevershall, the blackened brick buildings, the black slate roofs glistening their sharp edges" and other indications in this passage of shops along the hillside suggest the slopes of Eckington. But "the little market place" with the Sun "that called itself an inn, not a pub,"; "the church away to the left among black trees" and the pub names all indicate Eastwood. The positioning of The Miners Arms opposite the Mechanics Hall makes this very specific. Perhaps we must accept the village as a composite picture of Eckington, inspired by Lawrence's recent visit to that part of the country, and Eastwood, as he remembered it. The village gossip of Mrs. Bolton probably had its origins in his memories of Eastwood. We should think of Tevershall as a representative Midland village.

The Virgin and the Gypsy

Harry Moore in *The Intelligent Heart* noted that *The Virgin and the Gypsy* "similarly involved his (Lawrence's) recent visit to the stony landscapes of Derbyshire."

Certainly the village of Papplewick in the novel is described in great detail. "Past the gate went the whitish muddy road, crossing the stone bridge almost immediately, and winding in a curve up to the steep, clustering, stony, smoking northern village, that perched over the grim stone mills which Yvette could see ahead down the narrow valley, their tall chimneys long and erect".

"The rectory was on one side of the Papple, in the rather steep valley, the village was beyond and above, further down, on the other side the swift stream. At the back of the rectory the hill went up steep with a grove of dark, bare larches, through which the road disappeared."

But despite the detail it is difficult to identify the village with any certainty, although certain aspects of it, the mill and the stone bridge suggest Cromford.

What is certain is that the young people visited Chatsworth, one of the earliest 'ducal houses' to be open to the public. They appear to have travelled back via Bonsall (Bolehill), possibly visiting Wirksworth (Woodlinkin) and Ambergate in the course of the journey.

Drawn by Geoffrey Phillips

An artists reconstruction of the fireplace at Felley Mill.

Photo: By courtesy of Allan Hurst and Nottingham Playhouse

A scene from the Nottingham Playhouse production of 'The Daughter in Law' with Donald Gee as Luther and Cherith Mellor as Minnie Gascoigne.

D. H. Lawrence—Playwright

Lawrence wrote eight complete plays of which five have local setting: *A Collier's Friday Night* which was first published in 1934, although variously estimated as having been written between 1906, 1907 and about 1909; *The Daughter-in-Law,* 1912; *The Merry-go-Round,* 1912; *The Widowing of Mrs. Holroyd,* 1914 and *Touch and Go,* 1920.

In one sense they are disappointing reading as they present in dramatic form material which Lawrence has very frequently used elsewhere. But the extraordinary detail of their settings gives a valuable picture of miners' homes in Nottinghamshire at the beginning of the century.

Thus *A Collier's Friday Night* is set in "The kitchen or living-room of a working man's house. At the back a fire-place, with a large fire burning. On the left a rocking chair . . . the oven side of the stove . . . in a recess made by the fireplace, four shelves of books, the shelf-covers being of green serge, with woollen ball fringe, and the books being ill-assorted school books, with an edition of Lessing, florid in green and gilt, but tarnished . . . Under the window, a sofa, the bed covered with red chintz. By the side of the window, a quiver clothes-horse is outspread with the cotton articles which have been ironed, hanging to air. Under the outspread clothes is the door which communicates with the scullery and with the yard. On the right side of the fireplace, in the recess equivalent to that where the bookshelves stand, a long narrow window, and below it, a low, brown fixed cupboard, whose top forms a little sideboard, on which stand a large black enamel box of oil colours, and a similar japanned box of water colours, with Reeve's silver trade mark. There is also on the cupboard top a tall glass jar containing ragged pink chrysanthemums. On the right is a bookcase upon a chest of drawers. This piece of furniture is of stained, polished wood in imitation of mahogany . . . Between the little brown cupboard and the book case, an arm-chair, small, round, with many little staves; a comfortable chair such as is seen in many working class kitchens; it has a red chintz cushion. There is another Windsor chair on the other side of the bookcase. Over the mantle-piece, which is high, with brass candlesticks and two 'Coronation' tumblers in enamel, hangs a picture of Venice from one of Stead's Christmas numbers . . . The table is laid for tea . . . It is an oval mahogany table large enough to seat eight comfortably."

In *The Widowing of Mrs. Holroyd* the kitchen of a miner's small cottage lacks the cultural pretensions of books, paints and pictures, but shares with the previous room "a deep full red fire;" "a chintz-backed sofa under the window;" "a table with a red and blue check table cloth" and "On one side of the hearth . . . a wooden rocking chair, on the other an arm chair of round staves." It too is used as a place for drying off clothes and suffers from a plethora of doors. Lawrence's interiors have more exits and entrances than can have been dictated by dramatic necessity—doors to the scullery, the yard, the front of the house and the stairs. The kitchen is truly seen here as the centre of a house.

In these settings one glimpses some of the social rituals of the time—the women leaving the room while the men divide the week's earnings between them, the ritual of washing the pit dirt off the miner's back by the wife and the setting of the breakfast table while the snap bag and trousers are laid out in readiness for the morning.

Some of the pressing social problems of the time show through. *Touch and Go* tells us something of the tensions between men and masters in Eastwood, even using as its basis some of the characters, particularly Willie Hopkin whom Lawrence had known there. In *The Daughter-in-Law* Mrs. Gascoigne speaks of how this tension affected the community directly through strikes. "Meetin's ivry mornin'—crier for ever down th' street wi's bell—an' agitators. They say as Frazer dursn't venture out o' th' door. Watna' pit-top's bin afire, and there's a rigiment o' soldiers drillin' i' th' statutes ground—bits o' things they are, an' a' like a lot o' little monkeys i' their red coats . . . If you watch out fra' th' gardin end, you'll see 'em i' th' colliers' train goin' up th' line ter Watna'—wi' their red coats jammed i' th' winders. They say as Fraser's (the manager) got ten on 'em in's house ter guard him—an' they's sentinels at pit top, standin' wi' their guns, an' th' men crackin' their sides wi' laughing at 'em."

Here Mrs. Gascoigne mentions Watnall. She refers later to Heanor. Her son mentions free dinners at the Methodist Chapel. Specific places in the Eastwood locality are referred to elsewhere in the plays—in *The Daughter-in-Law* we hear of "living down Nethergreen" of the familiar Ram Inn and of shopping for furniture in Nottingham. It is perhaps in the representation of the disappearing Nottingham dialect that the plays are particularly interesting to Nottingham people. One could glimpse this in the passage on strikes quoted above from *The Daughter-in-Law*. But the play is alive with dialect words and phrases. "Clunch", "a pack of slutherers", "slormed," "Tha' has a bit too much chelp an' chunter . . . Tha' wort blortin' and bletherin' down at th' office," are only a few. The English language will be weaker for their loss.

Photo: Geoffrey Pugh

'Nottingham's New University' (the Trent Building).

D. H. Lawrence—Poet

Although Lawrence is now remembered chiefly as a novelist, when he first decided to write he confided to Jessie Chambers "I think it will be poetry". And it was his poetry that was first published in 1909 by Hueffer in *The English Review.* As Lawrence wrote in his introduction to his *Collected Poems* "many of the poems are so personal that in their fragmentary fashion, they make up a biography of an emotional and inner life."

One can, in fact, trace many of the early tensions of Lawrence's life in his poems. The fear felt by the children in hearing the sound of an ash tree blown in the wind mingling with the quarrelling voices of their parents is reflected in *Discord in Childhood* and refers to an actual ash tree. Similarly the poem *The Collier's Wife* refers to a situation familiar to Mrs. Lawrence when the news of an accident at the pit is brought to the miner's home, and the wife has to consider the situation.

"There's one thing, we s'ill 'ave a peaceful 'ouse f'r a bit,
Thank heaven for a peaceful house!
An' there's compensation sin' it's accident,
An' club money—I won't grouse.

An' a fork an' a spoon 'e'll want—an' what else?
Is'll never catch that train!
What a traipse it is, if a man gets hurt
I sh'd think 'e'll get right again."

The use of dialect here is interesting. Mrs. Lawrence never used it herself. The experience but not the style was hers.

Other facets of Lawrence's early life connected with The Haggs emerge in his poetry. The rabbit was a frightful pest to the Chambers. Lawrence records this in the lines

"Rabbits, handfuls of brown earth lie
Now, rounded on the mournful earth they have bitten to
the quick."

Another scene from the farm speaks of actual experience.

"Last night, when I went with the lantern, the sow was
grabbing her litter
With snarling red jaws; and I heard the cries
Of the new-born, and then, the old owl, then the bats that
flutter."

Particularly numerous among his early works too are poems addressed to his various girl friends, Miriam—Jessie Chambers, the girl of *Kisses on the Train*—Louise Burrows and Helen—Helen Corke of his Croydon days. The "bog end" to which he refers in an early poem was an actual place in Eastwood.

Lawrence did not come to poetry writing until he was twenty and his talent for it seems to me to have matured after he left Nottinghamshire, but the vividness of the few lines I have quoted suggests greater things to come.

From our point of view, though not from that of the poetry critic, Lawrence's poem on *Nottingham's New University* is interesting. It seems at the same time to be a vehicle for Lawrence's spleen and perhaps an attempt to carry on the quarrel that his grandfather, who numbered among his enemies William Booth, had had with Jesse Boot.

"In Nottingham, that dismal town
where I went to school and college
they've built a new university
for a new dispensation of knowledge

Built it most grand and cakely
out of the noble loot
derived from shrewd cash-chemistry
by good Sir Jesse Boot

Little I thought, when I was a lad
and turned my modest penny
over on Boot's Cash Chemists counter
That Jesse, by turning many

millions of similar honest pence
over, would make a pile
that would rise at last and blossom out
in grand and cakey style

into a university
where smart men would dispense
doses of smart cash-chemistry
in language of common-sense

That future Nottingham lads would be
cash chemically B.Sc.
that Nottingham lights would rise and say
by Boots I am B.A.

From this I learn, though I knew it before
that culture has her roots
in the deep dung of cash, and lore
is the last offshoot of Boots."

The Short Stories

"Do you know what I shall do when I am out of college? I shall write drivelling short stories and the like for money." So Lawrence wrote to Blanche Jennings in May, 1908. Taken in conjunction with his remark to Jessie Chambers on poetry it shows his uncertainty as to medium at the beginning of his career.

Lawrence wrote between sixty and seventy short stories, about a third of these were set in the Midlands. They fall into various categories and it is instructive to consider them thus.

One of the first things that emerges is that Lawrence had very little interest in the past. Only two of his short stories have an historical setting.

The first of these was an early one *A Fragment of Stained Glass* which describes the ruins of the old Priory* at Beauvale. "These ruins lie in a still rich meadow at the foot of the last fold of woodland, through whose oaks shines a blue of hyacinths, like water, in Maytime. Of the Abbey, there remains only the east wall of the chancel standing, a wild thick mass of ivy weighing one shoulder, while pigeons perch in the tracing of the lofty window." The description is still accurate to-day if one discounts the unromantic wooden props which support the walls.

This story recounts a legend told by the 'vicar of Beauvale' and in this perhaps reminds one of the local historian and Vicar of Greasley, the Reverend Rodolph von Hube who wrote Griseleia in Snotinghscire "an Illustrated History of the Earliest Times and from Reliable Sources" of his Parish.

The other story, set in the more recent past, was *Goose Fair.* The fair is still held annually in Nottingham on the first Thursday in October although it now takes place on the Forest not in the Market Place as Lawrence describes. The Poultry in the story refers to the east side of the Market Square, then a poultry market. Hollow Stone and the Lace Market are actual places on the route from Sneinton. The story tells of Saturday, October 8th, 1831, the day when news that Lord Grey's Reform Bill had been rejected by the House of Lords reached Nottingham on the last day of Goose Fair. Lawrence described the hardship felt in the town where "Trade, the invidious enemy; Trade, which thrust out its hand and shut the factory doors and pulled the stockingers off their seats, and left the web half-finished on the frame; Trade, which mysteriously choked up the sources of the rivulets of wealth, and blacker and more secret than a pestilence, starved the town." The story describes the Reform Riots in which Nottingham Castle was burned down.

The White Stocking is set in The Park, an Edwardian residential area just under the Castle. *The Primrose Path* is set in Nottingham and describes a journey from the old Victorian Station to Eastwood. These are the only two Lawrence stories set in modern Nottingham.

There are also two Derbyshire stories. *Wintry Peacock* was inspired by a dream Lawrence had whilst living in Middleton-by-Wirksworth. They share with the letters he wrote to Katherine Mansfield at that time an acute sensitivity to the winter landscape in

* The Priory is on private ground, but may be visited if you are given permission at the adjoining farm.

Derbyshire. The other is *Glad Ghosts* where we read that Lord Lathkill's place "was an old Derbyshire stone house at the end of the village of Middleton, a house with three sharp gables, set back not very far from the high road, with a gloomy moor for a park behind.

The green hills were dark, dark green, the stone fences seemed almost black. Even the little railway station, deep in the green, cleft hollow, was of stone and dark and cold and seemed in the underworld." A house very similar to this has been seen near the railway in Wirksworth by Lannah Coak and Moira Brown of the D. H. Lawrence Society.

One other short story, *Mr. Noon* is set in a village Lawrence calls Eakrast. He wrote "The school and the school house were one building. In the front the long schoolroom faced the road; at the back the house premises and garden looked to the fields and distant forest." In *Lawrence in Love,* Professor Boulton notes a postcard written by Louise Burrows "It's such a quaint place Eakring—red houses in trees like apples in foliage. The school house if attached to the school." S. M. Bircumshaw, however, identifies the setting with Eastwood.

But most of Lawrence's Midland short stories are set in Eastwood itself and the surrounding countryside.

Stories connected with the life of the miners were most numerous. They include *Odour of Chrysanthemums* set in Brinsley and repeating the same story as *The Widowing of Mrs. Holroyd; Fanny and Annie* which describes the Bennerley Ironworks and Princes Street Eastwood, and echoes *The Daughter-in-Law; Her Turn* and *Strike Pay* are concerned with the effects of the miners' strikes. The latter is obviously set in Eastwood with its references to the Primitive Methodist Chapel, the "squares of miners dwellings" and Scargill Street. *A Sick Collier* turns on the question of compensation for accidents and is reputedly based on an accident which occurred in Lawrence's time in Eastwood. *Jimmy and the Desperate Woman* deals with the Lawrentian theme of an intelligent woman trapped within a narrow mining community; *The Christening,* set in Princes Street also reflects this narrowness.

The wider Eastwood community is reflected in *You Touched Me* which is set in Meakins Pottery House in Lynn Croft and *The Horse Dealer's Daughter* set in "a small town . . . clustered like smouldering ash, a tower, a spire, a heap of low, raw, extinct houses." The Hollies was Eastwood House which stood on the Nottingham Road "on the left just after the Three Tuns Inn."

Outside Eastwood *Daughters of the Vicar* is set partly in Brinsley (Aldercar) and partly in Greasley (Graymeed). *Love among the Haystacks* is also set in Greasley and recalls haymaking with the Chambers family in Greasley fields.

"The two large fields lay on a hillside facing south . . . These two fields were four miles from the home farm. But they had been in the hands of the Wooleys for several generations, therefore the father kept them on, and everyone looked forward to the hay harvest at Greasley, it was a kind of picnic. They brought dinner and tea in the milk float which the father drove over in the morning. The lads and labourers cycled. Off and on, the harvest lasted for a fortnight . . . the high road from Alfreton to Nottingham ran at the foot of the fields." As in real life the fields lay just beneath a church in the story.

The Haggs Farm stories share both the themes and the description of his early novels. *A Modern Lover, Second Best,* and *Shades of Spring* with their landscapes of "large ponds . . . and far-off coal mines"; and "farms less than a hundred yards from the wood's edge" where "The wall of trees formed the fourth side to the open quadrangle" and field where "barley stood in rows, the straight blonde tresses of corn streaming on to the ground" all suggest the Chambers' home.

Interesting because it throws such vivid light on the experience of local travel in Lawrence's time is *Tickets Please* which deals with the workers on the "single line tramway system which boldly leaves the county town and plunges off into the black industrial countryside, up hill and down dale, through the long ugly villages of workmen's houses, over canals and railways, past churches perched high and nobly over the smoke and shadows, through stark grimy, cold little market places, lifting away in a rush past cinemas and shops down to the hollows where the colliers are, then up again, past a little rural church, under the ash trees on a rush to the terminus, the last little ugly place of industry, the cold little town that shivers on the edge of the wild, gloomy country beyond".

Photo: By courtesy of Granada Television

Jeanne Hepple portrays Annie in the Television adaptation of 'Tickets Please'.

Walk 1 The Urban Environment

Enter Eastwood on the B6010 from the A610 Bye Pass from Nottingham passing on the right of the scene of the Wakes by the Three Tuns Inn and the site of the now demolished Congregational Chapel and British Schools (where Lawrence was a pupil teacher) on the corner of Albert Street before turning right into Victoria Street.

A plaque denotes the house number 8a, where Lawrence was born. It is now a museum open every day April to October 10.00 a.m.-5.00 p.m., November to March 10.00 a.m.-4.00 p.m. (Closed 24 December to 1 January inclusive). Note the shop front where Mrs. Lawrence is said to have sold laces and baby clothes. The view down the hill shows the close proximity of town and country which is significant in Lawence's writings. The Squares, "great quadrangles of buildings on the hillside", which formerly stood lower down on the right of Victoria Street, have been demolished. However Princes Street at the foot of Victoria Street is virtually unchanged. Visitors who wish to do so may take a short cut from Princes Street down the footpath to Greenhills Road.

Otherwise return to the main road and turn right until one reaches "the tiny market place on the top of the hill, where four roads from Nottingham and Derby, Ilkeston and Mansfield meet". Lawrence frequently refers to the Sun Inn overlooking the market place.

Turn right down the A608 to Brinsley. On the left, going down the hill is The Miners Arms. Almost opposite is Phoenix Enterprises, formerly the Mechanics Institute. On the corner of Greenhills Road, also on the right are the Coal Board Offices where Lawrence collected his father's wages. Beyond them, on the left stands Eastwood Hall, the probable setting for the play *Touch and Go*. Just beyond this is Cockerhouse Road which appears as Shottle House Road in *Aaron's Rod*. The house and pit Lawrence described here have now gone.

At Brinsley look out for the small white cottage by the railway sideing referred to by Lawrence in a letter to Ralph Gardiner about *The Widowing of Mrs. Holroyd*. "Mrs. Holroyd was an aunt of mine—she lived in a tiny cottage just up the line from the railway crossing at Brinsley near Eastwood. My father was born in the cottage in the quarry hole just by Brinsley level crossing. But my uncle built the old cottage over again—all spoilt. There's a nice path goes down by the cottage and up the fields to Coney Grey farm—then round to Eastwood or Moorgreen, as you like".

Return along the footpath to The Breach. The new name for the house Lawrence lived in from 1987-91 is 28 Garden Road. The house, which has been restored by the Guild of Young Writers, is now open to

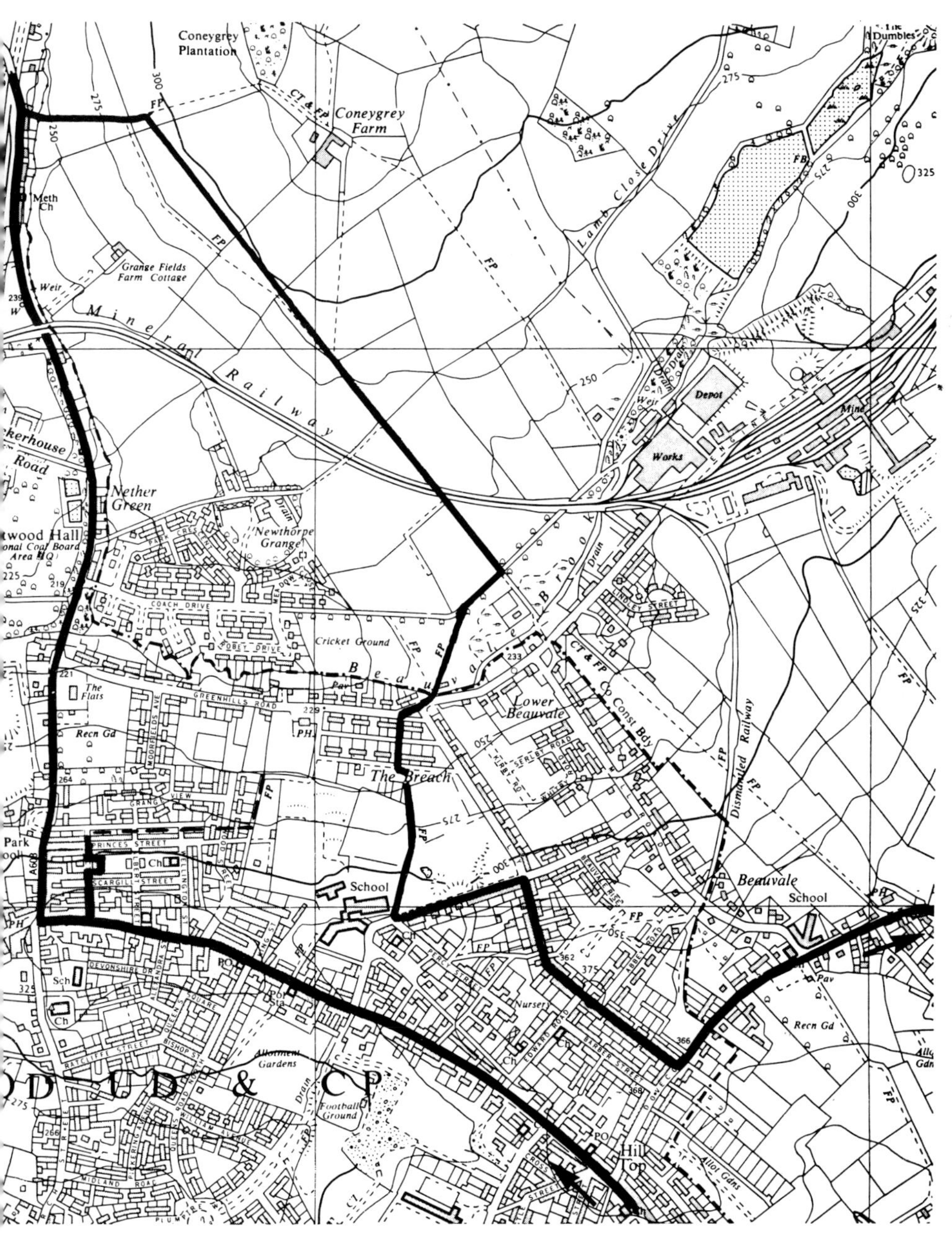

Reproduced from the Ordnance Survey Map with the sanction of the Controller of H.M. Stationery Office, Crown Copyright Reserved.

Allow 2 to 3 hours.

the public by prior arrangement with Mr. K. Roberts, telephone (0151) 653 8710.

Follow the footpath uphill across the open ground to Walker Street where the Lawrence's lived from 1892-1902. The exact house is not known as the dwellings were not numbered at that time. Exhaustive discussion in the Journal of the D. H. Lawrence Society (Vol. 1, no. 3, 1978) has failed to determine conclusively whether it is 8, 12 or even 10. Lawrence always referred to it as "the third house". From here one can see 'the country of my heart'.

The last of the Lawrence homes was 97 Lynn Croft Road. It is thought that the house described in *Aaron's Rod* was the other half of this pair of semi-detached houses.

On the return route to Nottingham look at Beauvale School which Lawrence attended and, on the right hand side of the road, opposite the new Ram Inn, the buildings of the original Ram Inn described in *The White Peacock*. In Greasley, on the B600, notice the old vicarage, and the fields which formed the setting for *Love among the Haystacks* and the haymaking scenes in *The White Peacock*.

Walk 2 The Country of My Heart

This is Miriam's country—the area associated with *The White Peacock* and *Sons and Lovers.*

Take the southern of the two roads to Felley Mill off the A608 noting on the right Haggs Farm, the former home of the Chambers' family. The buildings known to Lawrence lie below and slightly to the right of the new house. The whole area is private.

Felley Mill, now demolished, lay near the demolished farm buildings by the ford. 'The White Peacock Farm' according to Lawrence. Notice the pond high on the left of the path towards Annesley Hall—'Felley Mill pond', and the water-wheel chamber below the dam. This pond, originally much larger and containing two little islands is clearly the stretch of water described in 'Two islands' and 'Mooney' in *Women in Love.* The mill itself must have suggested Birkin's home.

The Old Quarry on the right of the footpath might have suggested the one where Annable was discovered.

Annesley Church, alongside the Hall, was the church described in the chapter 'Shadow in the Spring' in *The White Peacock.* It cannot be visited as it is unsafe.

It is possible in good weather to walk down the footpath from Felley to Moorgreen and thus pass through some of the countryside Lawrence loved best. Otherwise one should return to the main road and bearing left along the A600 for Nottingham, pause at the lodge gates just beyond Moorgreen Reservoir (the Willey Water of *Women in Love* and the Nethermere of *The White Peacock* and *Sons and Lovers).* The Lodge probably suggested Beauvale House in *The White Peacock.* On the opposite side of the causeway on rising ground one can glimpse Lambclose House (the Highclose of *The White Peacock* and the Shortlands in *Women in Love*). It is private property.

Felley Mill Pond. *Photo: By courtesy of the Nottinghamshire Local Studies Library*

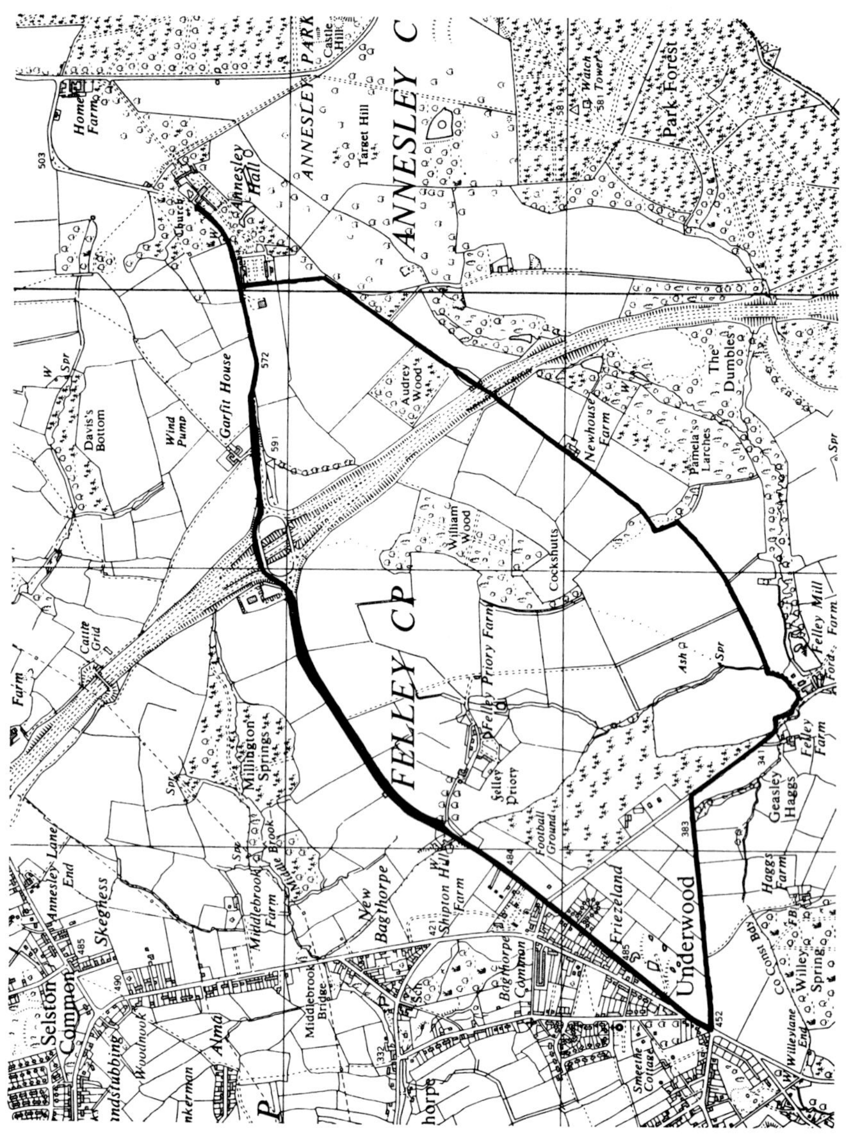

Reproduced from the Ordnance Survey Map with the sanction of the Controller of H.M. Stationery Office, Crown Copyright Reserved.

Allow 3 hours.

Walk 3 The Country of The Rainbow

The walk across Trowell Moor still gives one an impression of the unspoiled countryside Lawrence must have known.

Note the almshouses in the centre of Cossall. They are referred to in *The White Peacock* although other details of the village of Cossethay in this book do not refer to Cossall.

Cossall however is clearly the Cossethay of *The Rainbow*. The church is the one with which the Burrows family was connected. Louise Burrows is said to have provided a model for the character of Ursula Brangwen as did her father Alfred Burrows for William Brangwen. Note the Burrows' memorial windows in the church and the reredos carved by Alfred Burrows and his pupils in the parish rooms nearby. William Brangwen is described as using these rooms for teaching and woodwork in *The Rainbow.* Church Cottage is the Yew Cottage of the Book. It was the home of the Burrows family.

Marsh Farm stood where the modern bungalow Pipswood now stands just under the aqueduct where the road from Cossall meets the A6096 at Cossall Marsh. "The Brangwens had lived for generations on Marsh Farm, in the meadows where the Erewash twisted sluggishly through alder trees, separating Derbyshire from Nottinghamshire. Two miles away, a church tower stood on a hill, the houses of the little country town climbing assiduously up to it. Whenever one of the Brangwens in the fields lifted his head from his work, he saw the church tower at Ilkeston in the empty sky". Intrepid visitors should walk under the bridge and scramble up the embankment on the left by the disused colliery. From here they can see how it would have been possible for the aqueduct to flood the farm and thus drown Tom Brangwen. In good weather it is pleasant to walk back along the canal bank taking the first turning on the left back to Cossall. From this path the school, which the Brangwen children are described as attending, is clearly visible on the right.

The walk through Strelley is worth taking because, apart from the motorway, it seems unchanged.

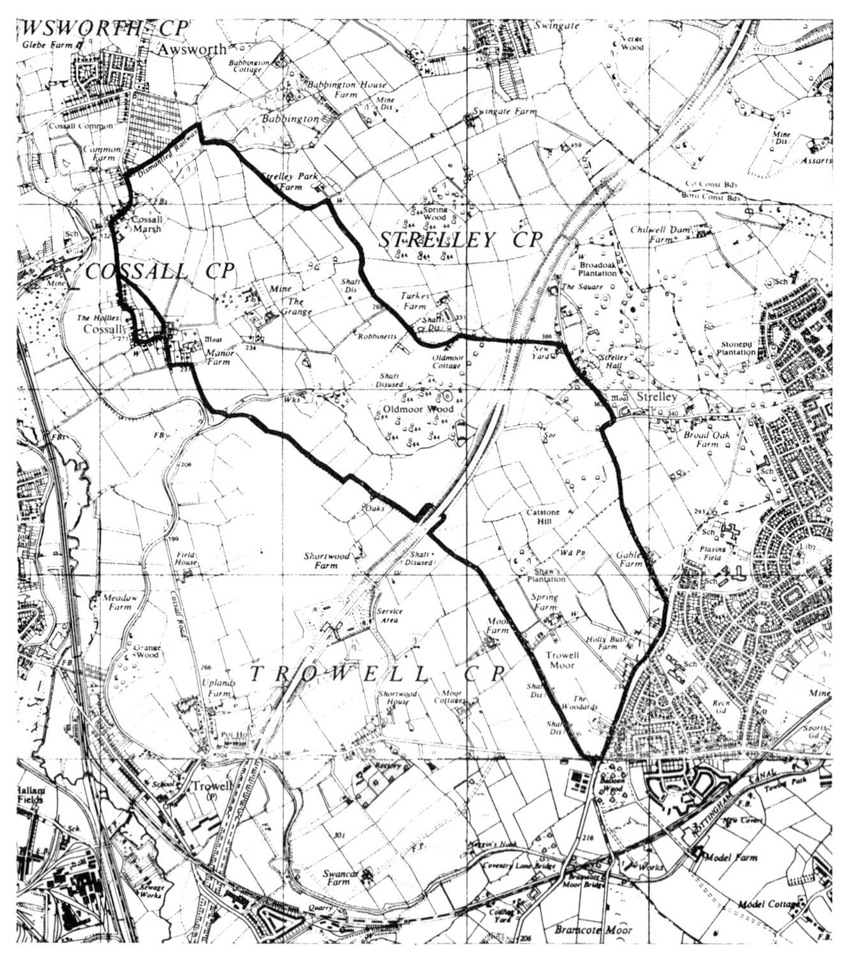

Reproduced from the Ordnance Survey Map with the sanction of the Controller of H.M. Stationery Office. Crown Copyright Reserved.

Allow 3 to 4 hours.

Walk 4 Lawrence's Nottingham

Nottingham has greatly changed since Lawrence's day. But there are several small areas which should be visited.

1. The area around the Castle

The narrow streets around the Castle still retain much of the atmosphere that Lawrence described in *Sons and Lovers* where Paul and his mother "turned up a narrow street that led to the Castle. It was gloomy and old-fashioned, having low dark shops and dark green house doors with brass knockers, and yellow-coloured doorstops projecting on to the pavements". This was Castle Gate. No. 9, Haywood's factory is described as Jordan's in *Sons and Lovers.* It was Lawrence's first place of employment. It has now been demolished. Visitors may like to visit the Costume Museum in this road.

Turning right out of Castle Gate as one comes from the city centre one should walk up Castle Road to the entrance to the Castle. From here one can see the 'Park Gates' mentioned in *The White Stocking* and see how "Above them the Castle Rock loomed grandly in the night". It is frequently mentioned in the novels. In *Sons and Lovers* it is aptly described as standing "on a bluff of brown, green bushed rock".

The Castle Museum was the place where Paul Morel's prize winning paintings were exhibited. It contains an Art Gallery. The view from the Castle is almost as Lawrence described it. "Away beyond the boulevard the thin stripes of the metals showed upon the railway track whose margin was crowded with little stacks of timber, besides which smoking toy engines fussed. Then the silver string of the canal lay at random among the black heaps. Beyond, the dwellings, very dense on the river flat, looked like black, poisonous herbage, in thick rows and crowded beds, stretching right away, broken now and then by taller plants, right to where the river glistened in a hieroglyph across the country. The steep scarp cliffs across the river looked puny".

Present day visitors might like to complete their tour by retracing their path down Castle Road (perhaps visiting the Brewhouse Yard Museum) turning left into Castle Boulevard and Canal Street and visiting the Canal Museum on the right of the road just before the junction with Carrington Street. If they bear right into Carrington Street they can still look over the parapet of the bridge and see the canal below them as Paul Morel did when he went to find work in Nottingham.

2. The central area around the Market Square

In *Sons and Lovers* Lawrence wrote "Over the big desolate space of the market-place the blue sky shimmered, and the granite cobbles of the paving glistened. Shops down the Long Row were deep in obscurity, and the shadow was full of colour. Just where the horse trams trundled across the market was a row of fruit stalls". The Flying Horse Hotel referred to in *The Lost Girl* is no longer there, although the name and the facade of the building has been retained for the shopping mall which replaces it.

John Heath

In order to see something of an earlier Nottingham visitors should walk through the Lace Market. In *Goose Fair* Lawrence gives us a picture of this area in the early nineteenth century. Trade was bad, warehouses were gutted by fire, the girl in the story drags her way up Hollow Stone through a Lace Market as 'quiet as the Sabbath' to take her geese to sell at Goose Fair in the area called The Poultry where Exchange Buildings now stand.

Paul Morel and Clara Dawes in *Sons and Lovers* also visited the area. Lawrence describes how "They threaded through the throng of church people. The organ was still sounding in St. Mary's . . . The large coloured windows glowed up in the night. The church was like a great lantern suspended. They went down Hollow Stone and he took the car for the Bridges".

Visitors may like to do the same, travelling down London Road to Trent Bridge and noting on the left the Cattle Market which Tom Brangwen visited with Anna Lensky in *The Rainbow.* They may profitably extend their journey by visiting Colwick Hall and Park, the site of pleasure gardens Tom Saxton and Meg visited on their wedding journey.

3. The area around the Forest

The now renovated Theatre Royal which Paul Morel visited with Clara Dawes makes a good starting point. Visitors should walk along North Sherwood Street. Behind the theatre was the Empire, the music-hall visited by Will Brangwen. At the junction of Goldsmith Street and Shakespeare Street, on the left-hand side are the old University College buildings. Lawrence was a student here. He describes Ursula Brangwen's college days here in *The Rainbow*.

Visitors should turn left along Shakespeare Street and then right into Waverley Street. On the right stands the Arboretum and above it the Nottingham Girl's High School which is described in *The Rainbow.* "The school itself has been a gentleman's house. Dark sombre lawns separated it from the dark select avenue. But its rooms were large and of good appearance, and from the back, one looked over lawns and shrubbery, over the trees and the grassy slopes of the Arboretum, to the town which heaped the hollow with its roof and cupolas and its shadows".

The Arboretum is worth seeing. On leaving it walk up Waverley Street and turn right into Forest Road. Nottingham High School, which Lawrence attended, stands on the right, continue to the junction with the Mansfield Road and return down the hill to the city centre. Lawrence, in *The White Peacock* described seeing "the square tower of my old school and the sharp proud spire of St. Andrew's here". On the left, at the foot of the hill, stands the Stakis Hotel where Meg and George had their wedding luncheon, although the name has been changed.

4. Dr. John Worthen has drawn my attention to the fact that Sneinton Market is the area described in Chapter 26 of *Women in Love.*

A Lawrence Tour into Derbyshire

Bramcote—The Hemlock Stone

Described in a walk in *Sons and Lovers* "They had expected a venerable and dignified monument. They found a little, gnarled, twisted stump of rock, something like a decayed mushroom, standing out pathetically on the side of a field.

"Everywhere in the field below, factory girls and lads were eating lunch or sporting about. Beyond was the garden of the old manor, it had yew hedges and thick clumps and borders of yellow crocuses round the lawn."

Cossall—See Walk 3

Ilkeston

Professor Harry Moore in 'The Intelligent Heart', mentions that Lawrence taught at the Wilmot Street Schoolroom off Bath Street—the main thoroughfare that goes uphill from the site of the old Railway Station to the Market Place.

Ripley

"We are here in Ripley—suffering rather. It is a cruel thing to go back into the past." Lawrence stayed here with his sister Ada Clarke at 10-14 Grosvenor Road. The shop is still there. Engines contemporary with Lawrence can be seen at the Midland Railway Centre at Butterley.

Alfreton

The church—visited by Paul and Miriam in *Sons and Lovers*

Wingfield Manor

Lawrence's 'favourite ruin'. "The manor is of hard, pale grey stone, and the outer walls are blank and calm . . .

'All eagerly paid their sixpences and went timidly through the fine clean arch of the inner courtyard. Here on the pavement, where the hall had been, an old thorn tree was budding. All kinds of strange openings and broken rooms were in the shadow around them."

"Round the broken top of the tower the ivy bushed out, old and handsome. They looked over miles and miles of wooden country, and country with gleams of pasture."

"The crypt underneath the manor was beautiful, and in perfect preservation."

Crich

"The straggling grey village of Crich, that lies high. Beyond the village was the famous Crich Stand that Paul could see from the garden at home. Great expanse of country spread around and below. The lads were eager to get to the top of the hill. It was capped by a round knoll, half of which was by now cut away and on the top of which stood an ancient monument, sturdy and squat . . .

'At their feet fell the precipice where the limestone was quarried away. Below was a jumble of hills and tiny villages, Matlock, Ambergate, Stoney Middleton."

The Tramway Museum here has trams such as Lawrence described in *Fares Please.*

Whatstandwell

"They went on, miles and miles, to Whatstandwell."

Cromford

Drive by way of the Via Gellia in order to pass Mountain Cottage.

Middleton-by-Wirksworth

Lawrence wrote in 1918 "I was up in the Midlands for a week last week—my sister negotiating for a little place for us—a bungalow on the brow of the steep valley at Via Gellia—near Cromford. We should have it furnished for a year—my sister (Ada Clarke) would pay for it—if the people agree to let. It is a nice place—with pleasant little grounds and two rough fields."

Photo: By courtesy of the Nottinghamshire Local Studies Library

Mountain Cottage. Middleton-by-Wirksworth.

The cottage he refers to is Mountain Cottage on the left as one climbs from the Via Gellia. This stay seems to have given Lawrence great pleasure. Possibly the story *Wintry Peacock* was inspired by his closeness to nature here. A letter written to Katherine Mansfield in 1919 illustrates this. "I climbed with my niece to the bare tops of the hills. Wonderful it is to see the footmarks on the snow—beautiful ropes of rabbit prints, trailing away over the brows; heavy hare marks; a fox, so sharp and dainty, going over the wall; birds with two feet that hop; very splendid straight advance of a pheasant; wood pigeons that are clumsy and move in flocks; splendid little leaping marks of weasels, coming along like a necklace chain of berries; odd little filigree of the field mice; the trail of a mole—it is astonishing what a world of wild creatures one feels round one, on the hills in the snow. From the height it is very beautiful. The upland is naked, white like silver and moving far into the distance, strange and muscular, with gleams like skin."

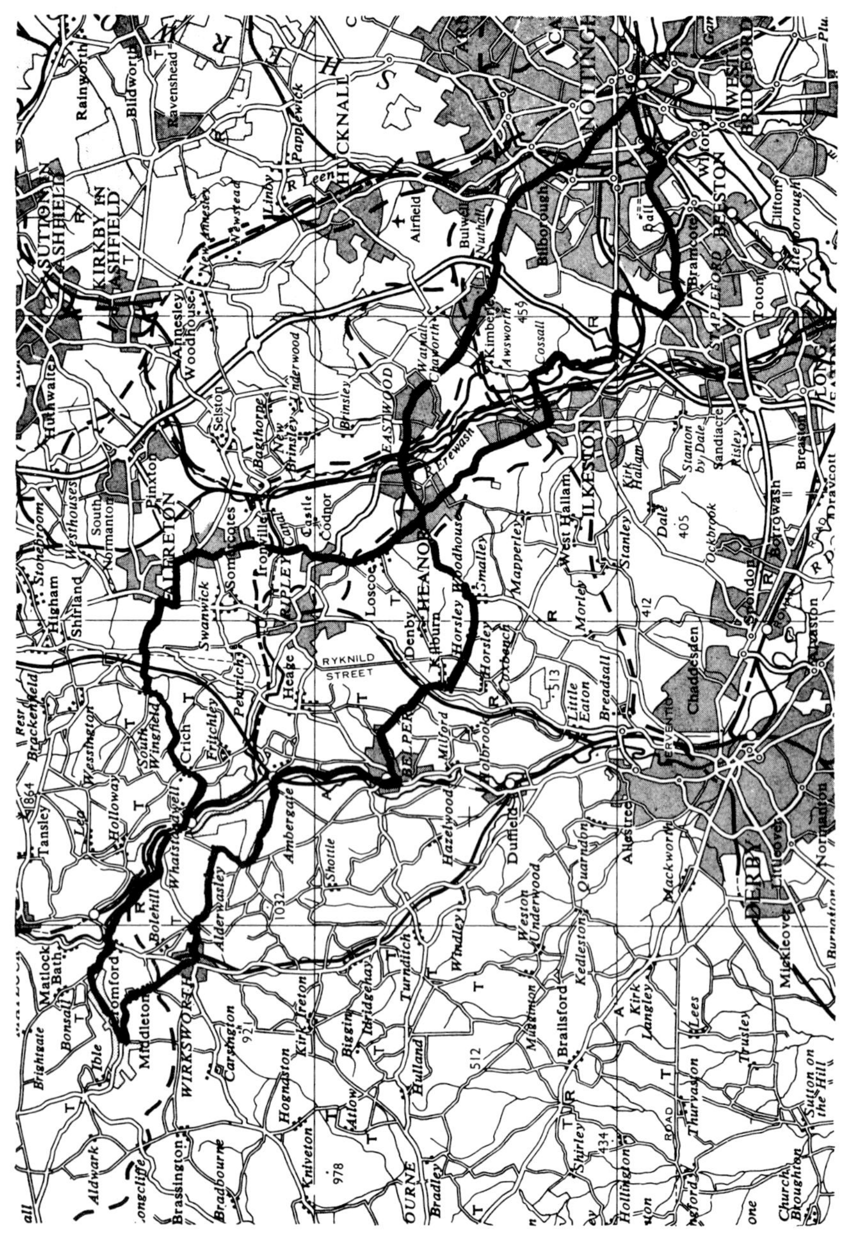

Reproduced from the Ordnance Survey Map with the sanction of the Controller of H.M. Stationery Office, Crown Copyright Reserved

Wirksworth

Home of the Beardsall's, Lawrence's mother's family. Alfred Brangwen's mistress was pictured as living here. "He found a beautiful cottage on the steep side of a hill looking clean over the town, that lay in the bottom of the basin, and away at the old quarries on the opposite side of the space."

Ambergate

Return point of the walk to Wingfield Manor in *Sons and Lovers.*

Langley Mill

Named in *Sons and Lovers*—Sethley Bridge—it is probably the township called Lumley in *The Lost Girl,* the place where James Houghton made his last abortive attempt to make his fortune by starting a cinematograph. "It was a long straggle of a dusty road down in the valley, with a pale-grey dust and spatter from the pottery, and big chimneys bellying forth black smoke right by the road. Then there was a short crossway, up which one saw the iron-foundry, a black and rusty place. A little further on was the railway junction, and beyond that more houses stretching to Hathersedge where the stocking factories were busy. Compared with Lumley, Woodhouse (Eastwood) whose church could be seen sticking up proudly and vulgarly on an eminence, above trees and meadow-slopes, was an idyllic heaven."

Postscript . . .

The interest in finding the original places in Lawrence's Nottinghamshire novels is matched by the fascination of the familiar game of finding the character. The identification of the real life counterparts of Lawrence's fictitious creations has been going on for a long time. In Nottingham Central Library, there are two interesting papers on the subject by S. M. Bircumshaw. The first is entitled *Women in Love—characters in the novel and persons they represent* and the second *Mr. Noon—characters in the story and the persons they represent and place names identified.* Each of them postulates names for the characters who might be regarded as suggesting Lawrence's people. The last section of *The Early Life of D. H. Lawrence* by Ada Clarke and Stuart Gelder contains 'A Note on the Proper Names in the Nottinghamshire Novels' which adds more to our knowledge.

Cossall Church

Photo: By courtesy of the Parochial Church Council

Now that most of Lawrence's contemporaries are dead there is little that is new that can be added to these identifications.

It is, however, an interesting exercise on the walks to look around and see the familiar names used by Lawrence over shops and on gravestones in local churches, and to discover that these too, like the place names, spring from 'the country of my heart.'